W9-BIP-178

EXPLORING THE HUMAN BODY

# The Lungs and Breathing

## Carol Ballard

**KIDHAVEN PRESS**

*An imprint of Thomson Gale, a part of The Thomson Corporation*

Detroit • New York • San Francisco • San Diego • New Haven, Conn. • Waterville, Maine • London • Munich

Produced by Arcturus Publishing Ltd,
26/27 Bickels Yard, 151–153 Bermondsey Street, London SE1 3HA

© 2005 Arcturus Publishing

Series concept: Alex Woolf
Editor: Alex Woolf
Designer: Peta Morey
Artwork: Michael Courtney
Picture researcher: Glass Onion Pictures
Consultant: Dr Kristina Routh

For more information, contact
KidHaven Press
27500 Drake Rd.
Farmington Hills, MI 48331-3535
Or you can visit our Internet site at http://www.gale.com

Picture Credits
Corbis: 11 (Nathan Benn).
Science Photo Library: 5 (BSIP Chassenet), 7 (Lea Paterson), 9 (CNRI),
12 (Prof. P. Motta, Department of Anatomy, University "La Sapienza", Rome), 15 (Coneyl
Jay), 17 (AJ Photo), 19 (Biophoto Associates), 20 (BSIP Jolyot),
21 (Philippe Gonier/Eurelios), 22 (Peter Scoones), 23 (Michael Donne),
25 (Chris Priest and Mark Clarke), 26 (Gusto Productions), 27 (Lea Paterson),
28 (Matt Meadows/Peter Arnold Inc.), 29 (Deep Light Productions).

**LIBRARY OF CONGRESS CATALOGING-IN-PUBLICATION DATA**

Ballard, Carol.
  The lungs and breathing / by Carol Ballard.
    p. cm. — (Exploring the human body)
  Includes bibliographical references and index.
  ISBN 0-7377-3020-X (hardcover : alk. paper)
  1. Breathing—Juvenile literature. 2. Lungs—Juvenile literature. I. Title. II. Series.
  QP121.B226 2005
  612.2—dc22
                                                    2004023215

Printed in Singapore

# Contents

# Why Do We Breathe?

From the moment you are born until the very last moment of your life, your body breathes. As you breathe in, air is sucked into your lungs. As you breathe out, air is pushed out of your lungs. This happens all the time, whatever you are doing. Whether you are awake or asleep, sitting still or running around, your lungs never stop breathing.

Humans, like many other animals, need to keep breathing all the time. If breathing stops, a person dies in just a few minutes. Breathing in provides our bodies with an essential gas called **oxygen**. Breathing out allows us to get rid of a waste gas called **carbon dioxide**. Breathing also allows us to talk, sing, and make other noises.

Breathing is also called **respiration**. It is carried out by parts of the body that together make up the **respiratory system**. These parts are all in the head and chest. They include the mouth and nose, throat, windpipe, and lungs. Other parts of the chest that play an important part in breathing are the **rib cage**, chest muscles, and the **diaphragm**.

**This diagram shows how the lungs and airways are positioned inside the chest.**

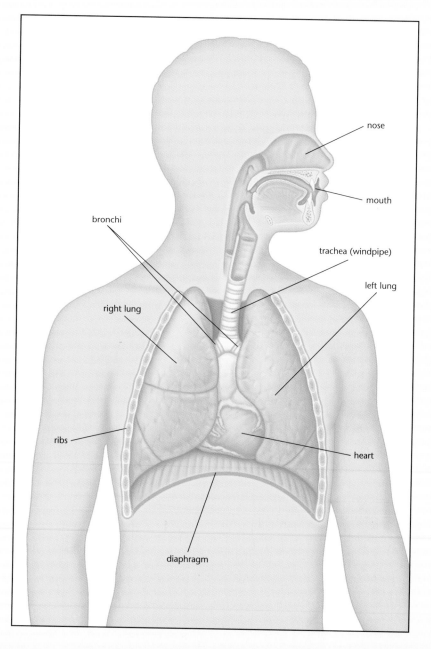

- nose
- mouth
- bronchi
- trachea (windpipe)
- left lung
- right lung
- ribs
- heart
- diaphragm

You need to take a deep breath to blow dandelion seeds away!

Sometimes our bodies need more oxygen than at other times, so we breathe in and out more quickly. Although breathing goes on all the time without our even thinking about it, we do have some control over our breathing. We can hold our breath for many seconds, for example, when we jump into a swimming pool. We can breathe in deeply and release the air slowly, for example, when we play a wind instrument. We can puff hard, for example when we blow out the candles on a birthday cake.

Our respiratory systems can sometimes make us produce strange noises! Whenever you cough or sneeze, hiccup, yawn, or snore, your respiratory system is involved.

## Case notes

### Why can't I breathe underwater?

If you try to breathe underwater, your airways fill up with water instead of air. Although water does contain oxygen, your lungs cannot work properly in water. Your body cannot get the oxygen it needs, and eventually you will drown.

Animals that live in water have special ways of overcoming this problem. Some, like whales and dolphins, come to the surface regularly to breathe in air. Others, like fish, do not have lungs. Instead, they have organs called **gills**, which are able to take oxygen out of water. Fish die without water in the same way that humans die without air.

# Nose and Smell

Your nose is the main route through which air enters and leaves your body. The nose is made from **cartilage**, a material similar to bone but softer and more flexible. The cartilage is attached to the bones of your skull. Together the cartilage and bone form a large air space called the **nasal cavity**. This cavity opens into the back of your mouth. It is divided into two by a wall of cartilage and bone, making your two nostrils.

When you breathe in, air is sucked into your nostrils. Hairs inside each nostril help trap dust and **microorganisms** in the air. This keeps them from getting any farther into your airways.

The lining of the nasal cavity produces a slimy fluid called **mucus**. Mucus also helps trap dust and microorganisms. The mucus trickles slowly down the back of the nose into the throat and is swallowed. When you have a cold, you produce extra mucus that you get rid of by blowing your nose.

**This drawing shows the structures that make up the nose.**

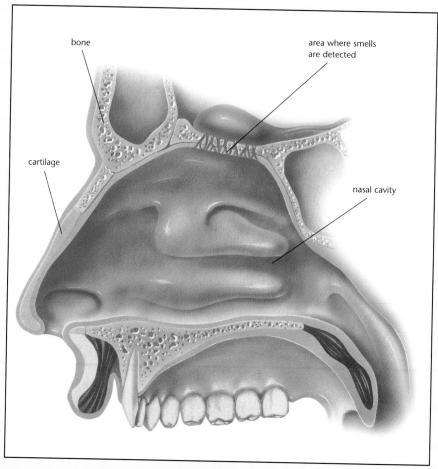

bone

area where smells are detected

cartilage

nasal cavity

The lining of the nose and nasal cavity has a lot of blood vessels running through it. The warm blood that flows through it helps warm the cold air as it enters your body.

Your nose plays an important part in allowing you to smell things. Air moves around in the nasal cavity when you breathe in. Chemicals in the air touch tiny hairs in the lining of the roof of the nasal cavity. These hairs send signals to the brain about the chemicals. The brain uses these signals to determine what the chemicals are, and therefore what you are smelling.

Humans can detect about ten thousand different smells!

The air around us contains so many different smells that it would be impossible for your brain to pick them all out. It only takes notice of those that are particularly nice (like perfume and flowers), those that are nasty (like blocked drains and dirty trash cans), or those that indicate danger (like smoke).

# Case notes

## Why can't I smell things when I have a cold?

If you have a bad cold, your nasal cavity gets blocked by mucus. This means that air cannot move around freely in the nasal cavity, and chemicals do not reach the tiny hairs. They do not send any signals to the brain—and so you cannot smell anything! Because your sense of smell is linked to your sense of taste, your food often seems less tasty when you have a cold.

# Sinuses

Not all the bones that make up your skull are solid.
Instead, some have air spaces inside them called **sinuses**.
These help make your skull lighter, and they also affect the
way your voice sounds. There are eight sinuses altogether,
four on each side of your head. They are linked to the nasal
cavity by air passages. Each sinus has the same sort of
lining as the nasal cavity. Just as in the nasal cavity, this
lining produces mucus.

There are eight sinuses in the bones that
make up your skull.

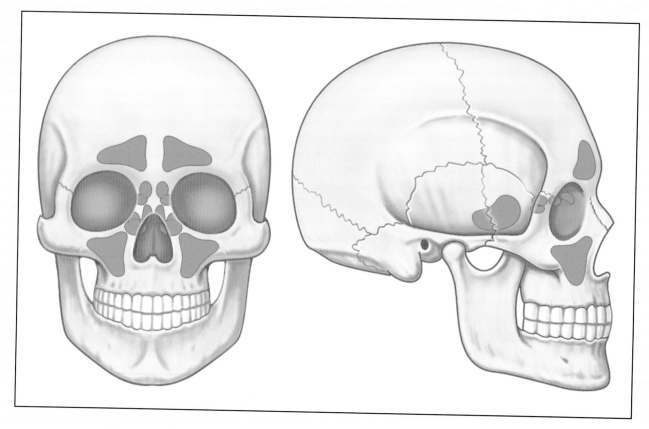

8

When you talk, air bounces around inside the sinuses and is amplified. This makes your voice sound louder and more interesting. Singers are trained to make use of this, so their voices sound really full and strong. When you have a bad cold, your voice often sounds duller than usual. This is because the sinuses are blocked with mucus, so air cannot move freely inside them.

The sinuses, nasal cavity, mouth, and ears are all linked, along with the **tonsils** and **adenoids**. If an infection develops in one place, it can easily spread to the others. People suffering from tonsillitis also often have ear infections and blocked sinuses at the same time. **Antibiotics** can be used to treat some infections. Sometimes an operation to remove the tonsils and adenoids can help.

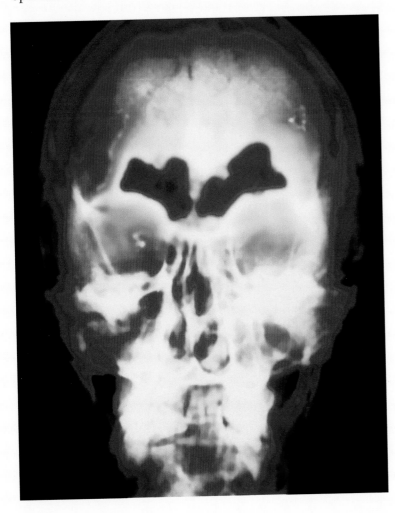

**An X-ray shows a person suffering from sinusitis.**

# Case notes

## What happens when sinuses get blocked?

If you have a bad cold or an allergy such as hay fever, the linings of the sinuses produce extra mucus. The linings can swell and become sore, making your head ache around your eyes. The extra mucus can block the sinuses and they may become infected. This is called sinusitis and can be very painful.

Decongestant tablets can help clear away the extra mucus. Sometimes blocked sinuses can be cleared by washing them out, but this should always be done by a doctor or nurse. If the blockage cannot be cleared in this way, a small operation may be necessary.

# Throat and Larynx

Once air has entered your nose, it moves down into your throat. The top part of your throat is called the **pharynx**. This is a hollow tube with strong muscular walls and a moist lining of mucus. Air travels from the nose and mouth, through the pharynx, to the **trachea** (windpipe).

Food also travels through the lower part of the pharynx. When you swallow, a flap of cartilage called the **epiglottis** moves down and blocks off the entrance to the trachea. This prevents food from getting into the airway. If you talk and eat at the same time, food may get into the trachea, making you cough to force it out again.

If you put your fingers gently on your throat and swallow, you will feel a lump move up and down. This is your **larynx**, or voice box, which is at the top of the trachea. It is made up from nine pieces of stiff cartilage that make a framework. The **vocal cords** are attached to this framework. When you breathe, air flows in and out between the vocal cords. They are apart, so the air flows freely and there is no noise.

**These diagrams show the vocal cords inside the cartilage framework.**

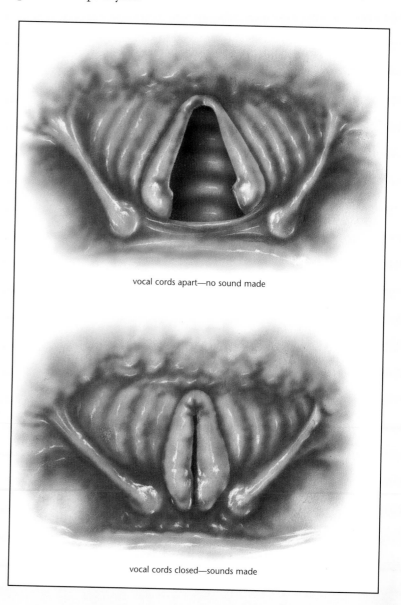

vocal cords apart—no sound made

vocal cords closed—sounds made

Your vocal cords allow you to speak, sing, and shout.

When you want to speak, neck muscles move the cartilage framework. This pulls the vocal cords tighter and closer together. As air flows through them, it makes the vocal cords vibrate, which makes a noise. The tighter the vocal cords are pulled, the higher the sounds they make.

The voices of young boys and girls do not sound very different. As boys become teenagers, though, their larynxes grow and their voices become deeper. Girls' larynxes grow much less, so their voices do not change much at all. Men have larger larynxes than women. Their vocal cords are also longer and thicker, which makes their voices deeper.

# Trachea and Bronchi

The part of the windpipe below the larynx is called the trachea. It runs down from the bottom of your throat into your chest. The trachea is a hollow tube, with walls made of muscles and fibers. These make it flexible, so that it can bend and stretch as you move your head and neck. Within the wall of the trachea is a column made of C-shaped rings of cartilage stacked on top of each other. These make the trachea strong and help keep it open.

Inside, the trachea has a moist mucus lining. Thousands of tiny hairs called cilia are attached to the lining. These wave backward and forward, trapping and removing dust and microorganisms from the air that you breathe in.

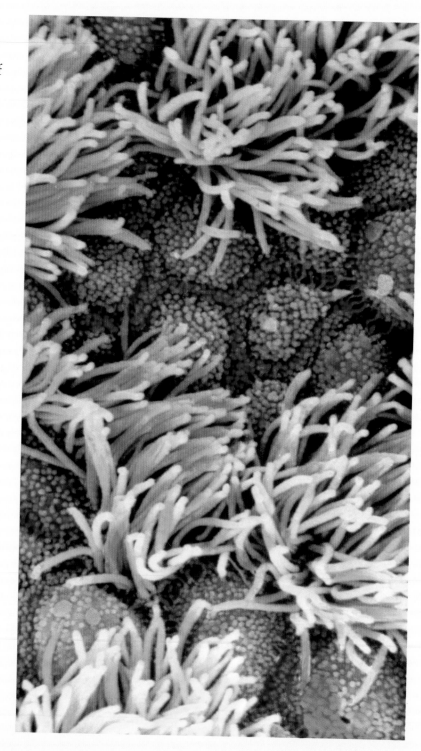

**This photograph was taken using a microscope. It shows the hairs on the lining of the trachea.**

12

The trachea branches into two narrower tubes, making an upside down Y shape. Each of the branches is called a **bronchus.** They are very similar to the trachea, with muscle and fiber walls and cartilage rings for support. The left bronchus leads into the left lung and the right bronchus leads into the right lung.

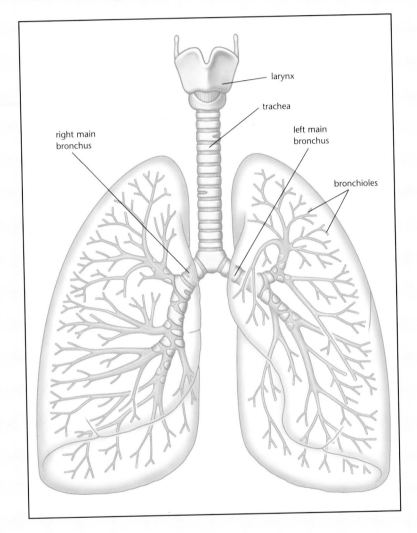

larynx

trachea

right main bronchus

left main bronchus

bronchioles

This diagram shows the trachea and the bronchi in the lungs.

Inside the lungs, each bronchus branches again and again, with the tubes getting narrower and narrower. The walls of the tubes gradually become more muscular and lose their cartilage rings. The tiniest tubes are called **bronchioles.**

If you took the trachea, bronchi, and all the bronchioles and turned them upside down, they would look a little like a tree. Scientists often call this the "bronchial tree."

# Lungs

Your lungs are two spongelike organs that take up most of the space inside your chest. Your ribs, spine, and breastbone form a bony cage that protects your lungs. The left lung is smaller than the right lung, because it has a hollow for the heart to sit in. Below the lungs is a strong, domed sheet of muscle called the diaphragm.

The left lung is made of two main parts, called lobes. The right lung has three lobes. The lungs are surrounded by thin layers called **pleural membranes**. A thin, slippery liquid lubricates these membranes, allowing them to move easily when you breathe. The left and right lungs are linked by the bronchi in the middle. **Blood vessels** and nerves also enter and leave each lung here.

The lungs have their own special loop of blood vessels. The **pulmonary** arteries carry blood from the heart to the lungs. (*Pulmonary* means "having to do with the lungs.") The pulmonary veins carry the blood back to the heart.

**This diagram shows air entering and leaving each lung through the bronchi and bronchioles, with a detailed view of the alveolus and capillaries.**

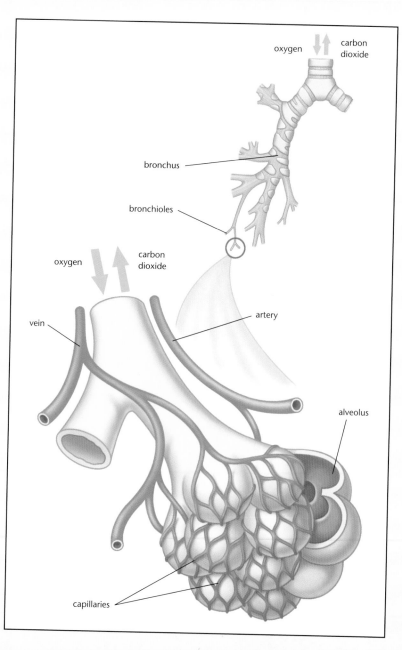

oxygen | carbon dioxide

bronchus

bronchioles

oxygen | carbon dioxide

vein

artery

alveolus

capillaries

Air enters and leaves each lung via the bronchi and bronchioles. The very narrowest bronchioles branch again to form even tinier tubes. At the end of each are round, hollow spaces called **alveoli**. These are clustered together at the end of the bronchiole like a bunch of grapes on a stalk.

Each alveolus is surrounded by a network of very thin blood vessels called capillaries. Inside, the lining of each alveolus is covered with a thin layer of fluid. This keeps the alveolar walls moist and also helps keep the alveoli from collapsing inward and sticking together.

The alveoli are almost too tiny to imagine. About 40 alveoli laid side by side would be .04 inch (1 millimeter) long. Altogether, there are more than 6 million alveoli in the lungs. If they were all opened out and fitted together, they would cover an area many times larger than your skin.

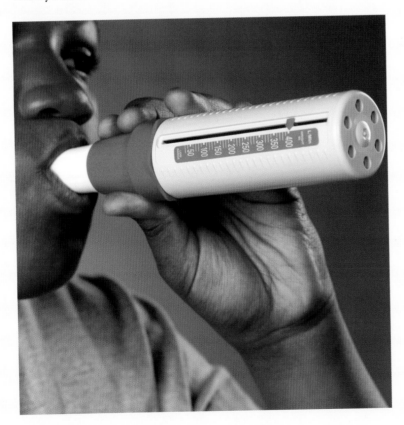

This machine is called a peak flow meter. It measures how fast you can breathe out.

## Case notes

### How much air can my lungs hold?

If a man takes a really deep breath, his lungs will hold about 6.43 quarts (6 liters) of air. Women's and children's lungs hold less. We rarely use the full capacity of our lungs. When you breathe normally, only about .53 quart (.5 liter) of air enters and leaves your body. When you exercise you breathe more deeply to take in more air. About 1.06 quarts (1 liter) of air is always left inside your lungs, even when you think you have squeezed out every last bit.

# Gas Exchange

Your body needs a constant supply of oxygen. It also needs to get rid of a waste gas called carbon dioxide. This gas exchange happens inside your lungs. Oxygen and carbon dioxide travel around your body in your blood. Blood with lots of oxygen is called oxygenated blood. Blood with little oxygen is called deoxygenated blood.

The pulmonary artery brings deoxygenated blood to the lungs from the heart. The deoxygenated blood travels through smaller and smaller blood vessels and at last reaches the capillaries around the alveoli. Blood capillaries are wrapped very closely around the alveoli. Both the blood vessels and the alveoli have very thin walls that gases can easily pass through.

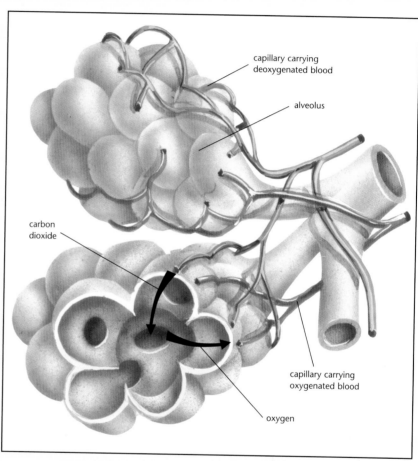

capillary carrying deoxygenated blood

alveolus

carbon dioxide

capillary carrying oxygenated blood

oxygen

**This drawing shows how gas exchange happens inside the alveoli.**

When you breathe in, the alveoli fill up with air. Oxygen moves from the space inside the alveoli, through the alveolar wall, through the blood capillary wall, and into the blood. It gets picked up and carried away by red blood cells. At the same time, carbon dioxide in the blood does the exact opposite. It passes out of the blood, through the capillary wall, through the alveolar wall, and into the space inside the alveoli. The carbon dioxide leaves the body when you breathe out.

The oxygenated blood is carried to your heart in the pulmonary vein. The heart then pumps it around the rest of the body, so that every organ and muscle receives a continuous supply of fresh oxygen. Organs and muscles constantly produce carbon dioxide, which is collected by the blood. This deoxygenated blood travels back to the heart and then to the lungs, where it loses carbon dioxide and collects oxygen. And so the process goes on and on and on!

The sticky tar from cigarette smoke blocks and damages the lungs.

## Case notes

### What does cigarette smoke do to people's lungs?

Cigarette smoke causes serious damage to the lungs. It contains tar vapor, which irritates the airways and causes infections. This destroys the tiny hairs inside the airways, so they cannot clean the air as it enters the lungs. Dirt, sticky tar, and mucus build up, and heavy smokers often cough a lot to clear them away. Eventually the alveoli become blocked and damaged, making it very hard to breathe. Cigarette smoke also contains a drug called nicotine. People who smoke become addicted to nicotine, so it can be very difficult to stop smoking. The best idea is never to start!

# Breathing Movements

If you put your hand on your chest and breathe in and out, you will feel your chest rising and falling. These are the normal movements that happen with every breath you take. Breathing in is called **inhaling** and breathing out is called **exhaling**.

When you inhale, several things happen together. The diaphragm contracts and becomes flatter. Muscles between the ribs contract, pulling the ribs and breastbone upward and outward. These movements make the space inside the chest bigger. The lungs are stretched, and air is sucked into them.

When you exhale, everything happens in reverse. The diaphragm relaxes and goes back to its domed shape. The muscles between the ribs relax, lowering the ribs and breastbone. This makes the chest space smaller, which squashes the lungs and forces air out of them.

**This drawing shows how the rib cage and diaphragm move as you breathe.**

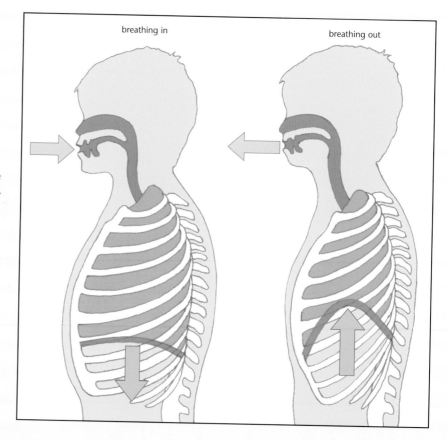

breathing in

breathing out

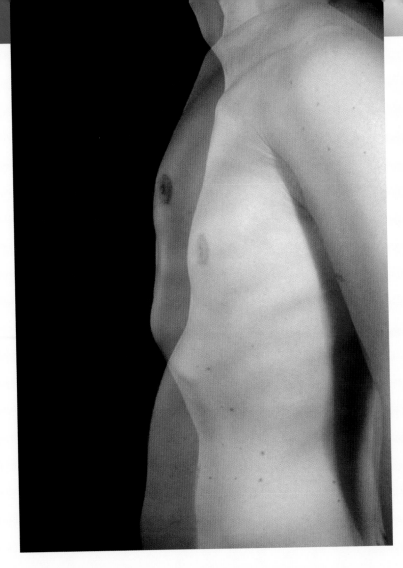

This photograph shows the positions of the chest and stomach when a person breathes in and out.

These movements happen all the time without your thinking about it. Your body settles into its own natural rhythm. When you are resting, you probably breathe in and out about twenty times in a minute. Adults breathe more slowly than this, and young babies breathe more quickly. It is not easy to measure how many breaths you take in a minute, because as soon as you start to think about it, it is hard to breathe normally.

When you exercise, your muscles need extra oxygen and they make extra carbon dioxide. This means that you need to breathe more quickly to speed up the process of gas exchange in the lungs. When you stop exercising, your breathing rate slowly goes back to normal. Sometimes, if you exercise very hard, you may get a pain in your side called a stitch. This is because the diaphragm has been working hard and, like any muscle, it needs a rest. The pain soon passes, and you can carry on again.

## Case notes

### What are hiccups?

Most people have suffered from hiccups at some time. They are uncontrollable and can be very annoying! They happen when your diaphragm makes a short, quick contraction that breaks the normal breathing rhythm. Air is sucked into the lungs so quickly that the epiglottis snaps shut with a "hic" sound.

# Controlling Breathing

Some things happen automatically in your body, such as your heartbeat, breathing, and digestion. These processes are vital for your survival. They happen every minute of every day, whether you are awake or asleep, running around or sitting quietly. They are controlled by a part of your brain called the brain stem. A tiny area in the brain stem, called the respiratory center, controls your breathing.

Our breathing rate speeds up when we exercise.

The respiratory center is connected to the chest muscles by nerves. These nerves carry signals from the brain to the muscles. To make you breathe in, the respiratory center sends signals to the breathing muscles to make them contract. This makes you breathe in. After a couple of seconds, the respiratory center stops sending signals. The breathing muscles relax and you breathe out.

The respiratory center normally keeps you breathing at a constant rate. Sometimes, though, you may need to speed up or slow down your breathing. When you exercise, nerves carry signals from muscles and joints to the respiratory center. These signals make the respiratory center speed up your breathing rate.

Sensors in the brain and arteries detect the amount of carbon dioxide in the blood and they tell the respiratory center. If there is too much, the respiratory center speeds up the breathing rate. The whole system keeps your body working perfectly.

Some activities, such as singing and playing wind instruments, need very careful breath control. It is also important in some sporting activities too, such as swimming and diving. People who take part in these activities often practice special exercises to help them control their breathing.

**Playing a brass instrument requires a lot of breath control.**

## Case notes

### Why can't I hold my breath forever?

However deep a breath you take, and however hard you try to hold it, you eventually have to let it go. This is because your body has a way to keep you safe. If you stop breathing, your body cannot work properly. Carbon dioxide builds up in the blood and your organs run short of oxygen. The respiratory center stops this from happening. It overrides your thoughts and makes you breathe normally again.

# Lack of Oxygen

Humans need a constant supply of oxygen to stay alive. Without oxygen, we die within minutes. When people are in conditions where there is a shortage of oxygen in the air, they need another oxygen supply. Also, people who have difficulty breathing may need help to ensure they get enough oxygen.

The world around us usually has air that is clean enough to breathe easily. In space and under water, though, there is no air to breathe. Astronauts need a supply of oxygen in their spacecraft. Divers need to take their own oxygen supply with them when they go deep-sea diving. They use tanks strapped to their backs.

Fish have gills to take oxygen from water.

Firefighters use their own air supplies to allow them to enter smoke-filled buildings. Without them, they would quickly be choked by the smoke. These air supplies also protect firefighters from any dangerous gases that may be produced by the fire.

Carbon monoxide is a gas. It is found in car exhaust and tobacco smoke and can also be produced by fires and faulty gas stoves. Carbon monoxide can take the place of oxygen in the blood, stopping the blood from carrying oxygen to organs and muscles. Small amounts of carbon monoxide can make you ill, but large amounts can be fatal. Many people have carbon monoxide detectors in their homes. These sound an alarm if there is carbon monoxide in the air.

Some illnesses can make it hard to breathe. People with such illnesses may use a mask attached to an oxygen supply that they fit over their mouth and nose. In serious cases, a mechanical ventilator can be used to pump oxygen into the lungs.

# Case notes

## How do astronauts breathe in space?

There is no oxygen in space, so astronauts need to take an oxygen supply with them. Inside a spacecraft, an atmosphere like that on Earth is maintained so that the astronauts can move around and breathe freely. If they venture outside the spacecraft, they wear a special spacesuit with oxygen cylinders attached. Carbon dioxide, water vapor, and any other gases are removed from the air the astronaut breathes out. The remaining oxygen is recycled to be used again.

# Asthma

Many people, especially children, suffer from **asthma**.
Asthma can cause coughing and wheezing and make
breathing difficult.

Asthma occurs when the bronchi and bronchioles
become inflamed. This makes their walls swell, so there
is less space inside them for air to flow through. Muscles
in the walls contract, narrowing
the space inside even more. The
bronchi also produce a lot of
sticky mucus that clogs them up.

Medicines for treating asthma
are often taken by using an
inhaler. Because there are several
kinds of asthma, people use
different types of inhalers. Some
inhalers, called relievers, are used
only to control a specific asthma
attack. They act quickly to
reverse the changes in the
bronchioles. Other inhalers,
called preventers, must be taken
regularly to control the
inflammation.

Never use somebody else's
inhaler—the medicines in it could
be harmful to you.

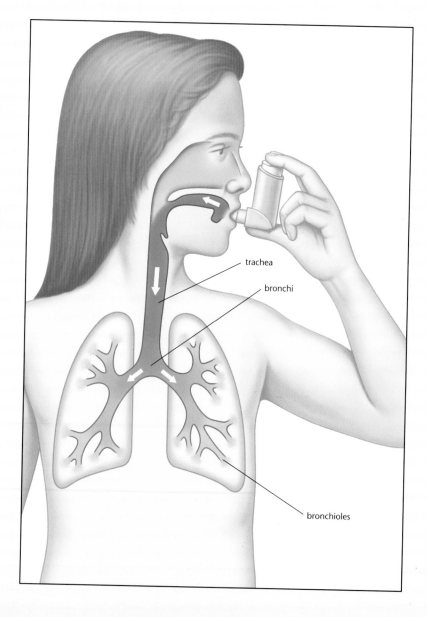

This diagram shows how medicines
from an inhaler spread into every part
of the airways.

trachea

bronchi

bronchioles

Using an inhaler can help prevent and control asthma.

## Case notes

### Does air pollution make asthma worse?

The air in towns and cities contains dust and dirt, together with gases from vehicle exhausts and factories. These things can irritate the linings of the airways. High levels of air pollution can trigger an asthma attack and can cause severe inflammation of the airways. Air pollution can also cause problems for many other people, including the elderly and people with breathing difficulties. Many television and radio stations now broadcast expected air pollution levels along with the weather forecast. This lets people take action to avoid breathing problems.

Sometimes an asthma attack may be so serious that it cannot be controlled just by using an inhaler. If this happens, emergency hospital treatment is needed. Medicines can be given to widen the airways and help the patient breathe more easily.

Different things cause asthma in different people. For many, it is triggered by an allergy to something in the air, such as pollen or animal fur. It can be set off when a sufferer eats or touches something to which he or she is allergic. Emotional upset and stress can also trigger an attack. Exercise can cause an asthma attack in some people.

# Coughs and Sneezes

When we cough, we force air out through the mouth very suddenly. It usually happens when we need to clear something like dust or mucus from the airways. A cough starts with a deep inhalation. Then muscles in the throat contract, trapping the air in the lungs. Muscles in the abdomen push upward, squashing the chest. When the throat muscles relax, the air is forced out very quickly, rattling the vocal cords as it rushes through.

When we sneeze, we force air out through the nose very suddenly. A sneeze is often triggered by dust or other particles in the air or by mucus inside the nose. The mechanism is similar to that of a cough. We breathe in, air is trapped in the lungs, the chest is squashed upward, and air is forced out at high speed through the nose.

**Using a tissue when you cough or sneeze stops your germs from spreading to other people.**

A yawn is an extra-deep breath and is usually a response to being tired or bored. Nobody is quite sure why we yawn. Many muscles in the face move when you yawn, making more blood move into the head and brain. This helps you feel more awake.

If you are still for a long time, your breathing may slow down so that your body does not get enough oxygen and

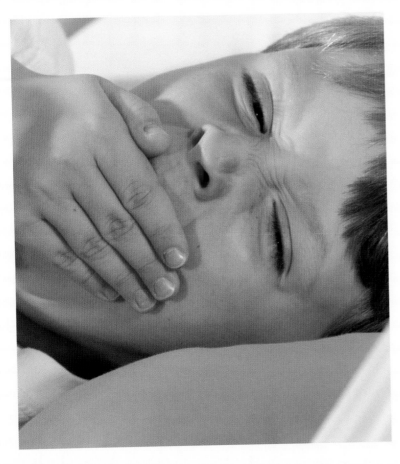

We often yawn when we are tired and sleepy.

extra carbon dioxide builds up. A yawn may help take care of this problem.

Snoring happens when air rattles through the nose and pharynx as you breathe in and out. Sleeping on your back usually makes snoring worse. Some people use special tape or clips on their noses to keep them from snoring. Others find that wearing acupuncture bands on their wrists while they sleep can help.

## Case notes

### What is hay fever?

Many people suffer from hay fever. Hay fever is unpleasant and can make you feel awful for a short while. It makes your eyes red and itchy. Your nose runs a lot, and you may have a bad headache. This is all because of an allergy to pollen. Some people are allergic to grass pollen, others to tree pollen, and others to particular flowers. Hay fever only lasts as long as the pollen to which you are allergic is being released.

# Artificial Breathing

Humans die without air, so anything that threatens our air supply is very dangerous. If someone stops breathing, it is important to get air into his or her lungs as quickly as possible.

The air that you breathe out contains more carbon dioxide and less oxygen than the air around you. There is still some oxygen in it, though, and it is enough to help a person who cannot breathe for himself or herself. By breathing your air into his or her lungs, you can save a person's life. This is often called giving the "kiss of life."

To do this, there are important steps that must be carried out in the correct order:

Using a dummy can provide excellent training for CPR.

❶ Lie the person on his or her back.
❷ Make sure there is nothing in the person's mouth to block the airway.
❸ Tip the person's head back to open the airway.
❹ Pinch his or her nose with your fingers to stop air from escaping.
❺ Breathe in.
❻ Seal your lips over the person's mouth and blow air into his or her lungs.
❼ Check that the person's chest rises as you blow.
❽ Move your mouth away so that air can escape from the person's lungs.
❾ Go back to step five and repeat, either until the person starts to breathe for himself or herself, or until medical help arrives.

Sometimes, a person's heart may stop beating too. By pressing the chest rhythmically in between each breath, trained first aid workers can keep both heart and lungs working for an unconscious person. This technique is called cardiopulmonary resuscitation (CPR). It saves many lives every year.

Some illnesses mean that a person cannot breathe at all. For example, if a person's chest muscles are paralyzed, his or her chest cannot move and so the normal breathing mechanism cannot work. An artificial lung is a machine that fits around the chest and does the work of the chest muscles. The first artificial lungs were large metal cases that enclosed the whole body except the head, but today some are no bigger than a backpack.

**This patient has a respirator to help him breathe.**

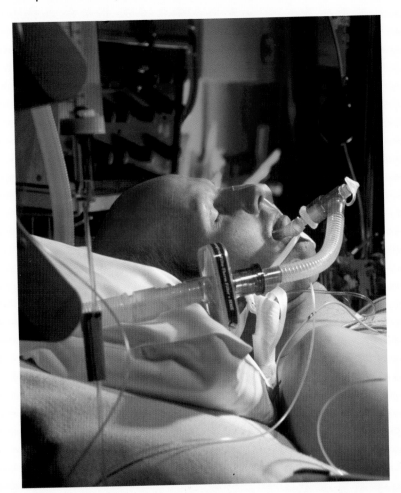

## Case notes

### How can I learn to do CPR?

Many organizations provide training in CPR, as well as other important first aid techniques. There are also courses for adults and young people. The Red Cross is a good place to start. You might find information about it, or other nearby organizations in the library or on the Internet. (For your own safety, always remember to ask an adult you know and trust before you agree to anything.)

# Glossary

**adenoids**   Small masses at the back of the nose involved in preventing infections.

**alveoli**   Tiny air sacs in the lungs (one is an alveolus).

**antibiotics**   Medicine used to cure bacterial infections.

**asthma**   A condition that causes breathing difficulties.

**blood vessels**   Tubes that carry blood around the body.

**bronchioles**   Small airways inside the lungs.

**bronchus**   A large airway between the trachea and lungs.

**carbon dioxide**   A waste gas that our bodies need to get rid of.

**cartilage**   Strong, flexible, bonelike material.

**diaphragm**   A sheet of muscle below the lungs.

**epiglottis**   A flap that covers the entrance to the airways when swallowing.

**exhaling**   Breathing out.

**gills**   Organs that underwater creatures use for breathing.

**inhaling**   Breathing in.

**larynx**   Voice box.

**microorganisms**   Tiny living things such as bacteria and viruses.

**mucus**   Thick fluid.

**nasal cavity**   The space inside the nose.

**oxygen**   A gas that is essential for life.

**pharynx**   The upper part of the throat.

**pleural membranes**   Layers surrounding the lungs.

**pulmonary**   Having to do with the lungs.

**respiration**   Breathing.

**respiratory system**   The organs that are involved with breathing.

**rib cage**   The bones surrounding the chest.

**sinuses**   Air spaces inside the skull.

**tonsils**   Small masses of tissue at the back of the throat involved in preventing infections.

**trachea**   The main airway to the lungs.

**vocal cords**   Bands of elastic fibers that vibrate to make a noise.

# For Further Information

## Books

Susan Dudley Gold, *The Respiratory System*. Berkeley Heights, NJ: Enslow, 2003.

Susan Heinrichs Gray, *The Respiratory System*. Chanhassen, MN: Child's World, 2004.

Chris Hayhurst, *The Lungs: Learning How We Breathe*. New York: Rosen, 2002.

Darlene Lauw, *The Human Body*. New York: Crabtree, 2003.

Suzanne LeVert, *The Lungs*. New York: Benchmark/Marshall Cavendish, 2002.

Anne Ylvisaker, *Your Lungs*. Mankato, MN: Bridgestone, 2002.

## Web Sites

**www.brainpop.com/health/index**
Click on "respiratory system."

**www.innerbody.com**
Click the picture of the cardiovascular system.

# Index

Page numbers in **bold** refer to illustrations.

adenoids 9, 30
air 4, 5, 6, 7, 9, 10, 11, 12, 15, 16, 18, 19, 22, 23, 24, 26, 27, 28
air pollution 25
airways **4**, 5, 6, 10, 13, 17, 25, 26, 28
allergies 9, 25, 27
alveoli **14**, 15, 16, **16**, 17, 30
antibiotics 9, 30
artificial lung 29
asthma 24–25, 30
astronauts 22, 23

babies 19
bacteria 11
blood 7, 14, 16, 17, 21, 23, 27
blood vessels 7, 14, 15, 16, 30
bone 6, **6**, 8
brain 7, 20, 21, 27
breastbone 14, 18
breathing 4, 5, 10, 15, **15**, 17, 18–19, **18**, **19**, 20, 21, 27, 28
   controlling breathing 5, 20–21
   breathing apparatus 22, 23, **23**
   breathing problems 23, 24, 25, 28, 29
   exhaling 4, 16, 18, 21, 28, 30
   inhaling 4, 6, 7, 12, 16, 18, 20, 26, 30
bronchi 4, 13, **13**, **14**, 15, 24, **24**, 30
bronchioles 13, **13**, **14**, 15, 24, **24**, 30

capillaries **14**, 15, 16
carbon dioxide 4, **14**, 16, **16**, 17, 19, 21, 23, 27, 28, 30
carbon monoxide 23
cardiopulmonary resuscitation

(CPR) **28**, 29
cartilage 6, **6**, 10, 11, 12, 13, 30
chest 4, 12, 14, 18, **19**, 26, 28, 29
chest muscles 4, 20, 29
cigarettes 11, 17, **17**
cilia 12, **12**
colds 6, 7, 9, 11
coughing 5, 10, 13, 17, 24, 26, **26**

diaphragm 4, **4**, 14, 18, **18**, 19, 30
divers 21, 22

ears 9
epiglottis 10, 19, 30
exercise 15, 19, **20**, 21, 25

fibers 12, 13
firefighters 23, **23**

gas exchange 16–17, 19
gills 5, **22**, 30

hay fever 9, 27
head 4, 9, 12, 27
heart **4**, 14, 16, 17, 29
hiccups 5, 19

infections 9, 17
inhalers 24, **24**, 25, **25**

"kiss of life" 28

laryngitis 11
larynx 10, 11, 12, **13**, 30
lungs 4, **4**, 5, 13, **13**, 14–15, 16, 17, 18, 26, 28, 29

mouth 4, **4**, 6, 9, 10, 26, 28
mucus 6, 7, 8, 9, 10, 12, 13, 17, 24, 26, 30
muscles 4, 10, 11, 12, 13, 17, 18, 19, 20, 21, 23, 24, 26, 27

nasal cavity 6, **6**, 7, 8, 9, 30
neck 11, 12

nerves 14, 20, 21
nicotine 17
nose 4, 4, 6–7, **6**, 10, 26, 27, 28
nostrils 6

oxygen 4, 5, **14**, 16, **16**, 17, 19, 21, 22, 23, 27, 28, 30

pharynx 10, 27, 30
pleural membranes 14, 30
pulmonary arteries 14, 16
pulmonary veins 14, 17

respiration breathing
respirator **29**
respiratory center 20, 21
respiratory system 4, 30
rib cage 4, **4**, 14, 18, **18**, 30

singing 4, 9, **11**, 21
sinuses 8–9, **8**, 30
sinusitis 9, **9**
skull 6, 8
smell **6**, 7, 7
sneezing 5, 26, **26**
snoring 5, 26, 27
spine 14
stitch 19
swallowing 6, 10, 13

talking 4, 9, 10, 11
throat 4, 6, 10, 11, 12, 13, 26
tonsillitis 9
tonsils 9, 30
trachea 4, 10, 12–13, **12**, **13**, **24**, 30

vocal cords 10, **10**, 11, 26, 30
voice 8, 9, 11
voice box *see* larynx

wind instruments 5, 21, **21**
windpipe *see* trachea

yawning 5, 26, 27, **27**